Andrew Fusek Peters and Polly Peters are highly
esteemed authors and editors. Between them, they
have produced over forty critically acclaimed titles;
storybooks, picture books, graphic novels,
anthologies and poetry collections. 'Poems With
Attitude' and 'Poems With Attitude Uncensored'
were both Guardian Education book of the week.

"It is rare and welcome to find a collection that
speaks so directly to teenagers" The Guardian
"the poems are brilliant" School Librarian
"sharply apposite poems... a real book for teenagers
and probably not to be read by faint-hearted
adults!" Carousel

Andrew's graphic novel, 'Ed and the Witchblood',
was also Guardian Education book of the week. The
sequel to this is 'Ed and the River of the Damned'.

Andrew and Polly are currently working on fiction for
young adults. They have also recorded a CD of their
teenage poetry for 'The Poetry Archive'. You can
find out more information about their books on
www.tallpoet.com.

'Crash' is dedicated to all those who
have ever placed flowers
by the roadside

CHARACTERS

Nat (Nathan) Newbery – Age 17
(born Nathaniel Herrick) Birthdate: 2nd April.
Studying: English Lang/Lit combined, Music, History, Psychology AS levels at Ludham College.
Main pastime: writing and arranging songs. Lead vocalist/lead guitarist in band 'Stormboy'.
Brief history: adopted aged 11 months.

Carl Archibold – Age 17
Birthdate: 7th September.
Studying: GNVQ Intermediate Business at Ludham College.
Main pastime: bass player in band 'Stormboy'. Collects examples of atrocious puns for future use. Best mates with Nat.
Brief history: farmer's son, youngest of three boys.

Kate Cottam – Age 16
Birthdate: 12th December.
Studying: GCSE at Priestcastle Community High School. (Going on to Ludham College.)
Favourite subjects: Performing Arts, English and PE.
Main pastimes: solo distance swimming and drama. Intends to do BTEC in performing arts.
Brief history: only child.

Will Hunter – Age 34. Occupation: Photocopier engineer.

Occasional appearances by:
Buzzard
PC Laura Snead
Mrs Juliet Newbery (Nat's Mother)
Mr Frederick Newbery (Nat's Father)

CARL – BACKSTAGE NERVES

Maybe I should have an operation
To surgically graft my bladder to the nearest toilet.
In fact,
I might almost be accused of having intimate relations
With a loo,
The amount of times I've been
In and out
In the last few minutes.
Me? Nervous?
Let's just say, when it comes to the shakes
I beat any alcoholic hands down
And I just have a tiny worry
That the electrics/the band/MY LIFE will fall apart
In the next fifteen minutes.

Kate – Considering the impact 1

Considering it's pouring down outside,
In here is hot;
Heavy with slurring smoke and bass.
The band are nearly ready.
Shall I stay?
Or rush to make the bus
Since Sue's quite clearly otherwise engaged!
Might just as well have come here
By myself
For all the girly banter I'm now spared.

But,
Considering it's pouring down outside,
In here is warm
And music is a fog.

Kate – Considering the impact 2

This fog of sound,
Odd lullaby that dulls until lights dim.
A hoverfly of spotlight
On the singer
Seems to lift him from the dusty stage.
A moth perhaps
And then the first chords rush to fill the space.
A voice that comes from –
Where?
Spins broken bridges in the air
And I'm aware
I want to cross.

Who is he? Where's he from?
What's his name?
Don't move! I want to still, distil
Freeze-frame, preserve
Stand here and listen in a
Never-ending loop.

He sings "I'm on the outside, looking in"
And that is me
Here looking, standing at the edge
Observing and considering
The body-blow
Of impact
That is him.

So, considering I nearly didn't stay,
Thank God for rain!

NAT – LEAD SINGER OF "STORMBOY"

Sings: On The Outside

I'm the wall without a door
I'm the country got no law,
I'm the forest without a tree
Growin' nowhere, set me free!

Got my body from the tip,
Stole my heart from the rusty skip,
Clothes were flown in by the storm
Praise the devil, Let's perform!

I'm on the outside lookin' in
LOOKIN' IN
Prayin' that they'll let me in
LET ME IN
Don't know if I got what it takes
WHAT IT TAKES
In this street life full of fakes
FULL OF FA-A-A-A-AKES

Cos I'm the shop without no goods,
Road that's lost it in the woods,
I'm the ship without a sea
Drownin' in this history

Got my lungs from the corner store,
Mouth and lips from the lion's roar,
Words I snatched from the sky,
Time for this song to get high!

I'm on the outside lookin' in
LOOKIN' IN
Prayin that they'll let me in
LET ME IN
Don't know if I got what it takes
WHAT IT TAKES
In this street life full of fakes
FULL OF FA-A-A-KES

NAT – MAKING HISTORY

Humming
'In this street life full of fakes…'

Just turned seventeen, in a band, studies going well,
When the truth reappeared to break the spell.
I call them 'Mum' & 'Dad' and sure, they're great
But they're not the names on my birth certificate.
I've always known I wasn't theirs, but felt at home
Loved for being me and me alone,
Though I've grown up feeling I don't quite fit,
Jigsaw Nat with a missing bit.
Well, all through the years, they've let me look
At what passes for my real 'life story book':
A scrap-book with fragments of the tiny me,
Brief facts to furnish my history.
But I'd never really registered how
My birth-mum was the exact age I am now.
Names and dates I had formerly read
Triggered a hurricane in my head.
Passed through time from pillar to post,
Up pops Nat like a piece of toast,
Birth mum, foster parents – new Dad and Mum,
I had to find more about from where I'd come.

I couldn't stand to wait for another year
Till all the legal routes click into gear;
So on the web I searched by night,
Found a number and filled with such fright,
Rang, ready with some story to play for time,
To give me a chance to spin a line.
A woman answered.
"Is... Judith there?"
"Oh, not any more love,
 was she the one with the long brown hair?
 Let me think, you could try her sister..."
I laughed! Success! I could almost have kissed her!
But when I made that second call and spoke,
Revealed I was her sister's son, my newfound aunt broke
Down in tears and told this tale to me
Of Nathaniel Herrick's history –

"A girl called Judith, sweet sixteen
Walked out with the best looking lad on the scene
But one night in the back of his car,
Our local boy went just too far.
Said he'd stay, but when the child arrived
Well, Nat, you just cried and cried and cried,
Which babies do, that's just a fact
An excuse for a dad-disappearing act.

Your mum, she really tried, but love and hope
Were stolen and my older sister could not cope.
She fell apart with desperation,
The doctor gave her medication...
She wanted the best for her little lad.
What she did, forgive her, it wasn't bad....

But bad in her life eventually turned to worse
And two years ago...leukaemia took her like a curse."

She sobbed as I put down the phone
And Nat is more, not less alone.
A father: Billy, who didn't know how to care
Vanished like mist in the morning air,
Leaving like a footprint, only a name,
Play on this dark detective game...

CARL – THE GIG

We had a crowd! No-one threw bottles!
They even moved around (a bit)!
It beats drunken Young Farmers any day.
I'm no farmer for life –
My good bloke of a dad is knackered, the price of lambs
   a joke,
And I'm sorry but pulling ewes and their young apart,
(the fields filled with screaming all night),
And calling it weaning,
Is not for me in the long run.
I'm not naïve. Rock stardom isn't waiting
in a stretch limo round the corner.
For a start, it's too muddy round here,
And apart from Nat,
We aren't exactly studded with sex-appeal.
No, it's study, study, study.
Exams, more exams, pro-plus-late-nighters
And the dream of a career.
They keep telling my dad to diversify.
But people still need wool.
And something dead to get their teeth around on a Sunday.
Dad has no desire to set up a sodding butterfly farm,
Or get-to-know-EWE-better therapy sessions...
What a bleating life. At least I'm in with a chance.
That was some gig. I slapped that bass,
The girls were smiling.
We had a crowd.

15

NAT – ENTER STAGE LEFT

To be what I am not is what I do...
Carl took one look inside, then laughed and blew
Me off. So, here I am alone in Drama Club,
And here, I am not Nat. Ay, there's the rub,
As when we play our warm-up trusting game,
It fits that I don't wear my birthright name.
Let go, join in, have a bit of fun,
Adopt a mask, a pose, a character...a son.

I stood on a chair, then closed my eyes and fell
Into six pairs of arms, the last of which... well
I was blown away, opening my cynic eyes,
Found to my dumbfounded surprise,
Such loveliness, I lost all tact,
Stammered, blushed, forgot my act,
She helped me stand, this was no game
As I was caught in her freeze-frame.

Kate – At the Swimming Pool

When I'm in water
The outer clamour clears.
My thoughts can swim,
Where hands are fins
To cut the shadowed light.
Slow and steady as walking pace…
To swim is to breathe.
Twenty lengths and counting,
Feeling great,
Away from stress and school, exams.
Each time I turn my head
and hold my breath away from air,
I can see his face,
See each moment
Frame by frozen frame.
And now he has a name: Nat.
The outside boy, the voice, the song,
Who gatecrashed drama club.
Last night, ten minutes in,
The creak of door
"Er, sorry I'm late…is this the right place?
I was, wondering about, um, joining up."
Him, in the doorway, with the corridor lights behind
Like some perfectly timed stage moment,
He wore the neon like a flaming cloak.

NAT & CARL – *SQUASH CLUB CHANGING ROOMS*

NAT: This girl I met in drama club…

CARL: Does she perform?

NAT: She's really fit.

CARL: Nice one, mate.

NAT: No, she's really fit.

CARL: I believe you, you lucky, lucky boy.

NAT: You don't understand.

CARL: I do. Oh yes, yes, more, more, yes!

NAT: I could really brain you sometimes. As in give you a brain.

CARL: Oh bleat me with your big stick Nat, I'm just a poor hill farmer's boy.

NAT: There's a song in that! quick where's my pen?… No you moron.

She's into swimming. She is fit in the true sense of the word.

CARL: And you're up for taking the plunge?

NAT: What is it with you and puns? Here am I opening up to you…

CARL: I bet you'd like to give her a length.

NAT: That's it! I was going to talk about how well
   we got on,

and chatted and how we're going to meet up next week,
   the day after drama

and I'm nervous and all that, but forget it.

CARL: Sorry Nat. Good luck. Chuck your fears in the
   deep end.

I'm just a jealous sheep mucker. You go for it.

You have my baa baa baalessing.

NAT - TONE ALONE

The phone goes, let it lead me
To where I want to go.
Pocket full of life and change,
You've really got to know

I pray, you say you're not engaged
Nor busy on the line,
'Cos I got your sexy number
And you make me feel so fine.

I'LL LOOK YOU UP UNDER LOVE,
LET THESE FINGERS DO THE WALKIN'.
YELLOW PAGES ALL A FLUTTER,
GOT NO ANSWER, KEEP ON TALKIN'.

So listen, Mrs Operator,
Gotta make this thing direct,
Press the button, give me credit,
I just wanna reconnect.

I'm payin' for love as I go
You top me up, so I can't fail,
Feelin' healin' your vibration,
Tells me that I got voice mail.

I'LL LOOK YOU UP UNDER LOVE,
LET THESE FINGERS DO THE WALKIN'.
YELLOW PAGES ALL A FLUTTER,
GOT NO ANSWER, KEEP ON TALKIN'
KEEP ON TALKIN'
KEEP ON TALKIN'
KEEP ON TALKIN'.

NAT – IT WENT SWIMMINGLY

"It's a bit hot in here! Very stiffy, I mean, stuffy…"

We went for a swim. Not a good idea –
I was crawling to catch up, but let's make this clear;
The only reason she slaughtered me,
Was a common case of manly courtesy.
Wrapped in cling-film, she exited the pool,
And the effect on my body was somewhat cruel.
You could say it was natural, not bad but good
When part of me didn't do what it should.
I crossed my legs and stammered about
Doing one more length. Without a doubt
She was slightly embarrassed, but shared the joke,
As all I could think of was doing the breaststroke.

Kate – Nerves

It's way too hot and these jeans cut in
But at least exams are done.
Have I got enough cash? And what's the time?
Is he here already? Damn.
Hate being early, hands feel sweaty.
This jacket is wrong: too hot.
Can't breathe with the thought
He'll be here in a minute
Walking towards me…I hope.
This feels like real drama,
Not the Thursday night stuff
Of masks and making up
But seeing his face, alone,
those eyes that burn.
Did we really say 7.00? Have I got the right time?
What if he's forgotten?
What if, after he saw me swimming,
He decided to call it off? Though he seemed fine at Drama?
What if he simply doesn't turn up;

He's lost, he's late, not bothered?
Good God! Get a grip!
Sack the committee in your head!
Slow down the breathing,
Think about water. Stop.
Look at the kerbstones, look at the posters,
Try to look cool and calm, porpoiseful...
But what do I say when he does get here? Do the
  nonchalant,

The don't-care, hard-to-get, enemy-of-keen?
Oh forget it, Kate, face the facts,
He simply isn't coming...probably laughing with that
  mate of his about
Little old Kate-In-Wait...
What a git, that pompous, macho, too damn gorgeous,
  self-esteem-stabbing...

Oh! Hiya Nat!

NAT – IT COULD ONLY HAPPEN IN A MOVIE

Went to a film, bit of a cliché, but hey,
Considering my nerves, it went OK.
Felt like I was twelve again, not sure what to do,
Machine-gun stammering "a…a…after you!"
Sank into seats, the lights went low,
Come on Nat, just go with the flow.
Just as courage was growing bolder,
Her arm slipped around **my** shoulder!
Easy-peasy as jumping off a log,
Suddenly tongue-tied glorious snog!
And as for normally slapped down hands,
They managed to climb the Northern lands,
But heading South, the advances gained,
Were driven back. I was restrained.

Typical boy, forever in a rush,
Going too far in a first night crush.
Had this boy blown it? Would Kate turn cold?
But her smile was priceless, and I was sold.
She held my hand, as we walked away
Considering my nerves, it went OK.

NAT & Kate – A GREAT TEXT LIFE

LNG TYM NO C!
FREE 2 TLK?
KATE

AS A MTR OF FCT
IM UNDR YR SPL
LOTS OF LUV
NAT

IT WUD B GR8
2 AV A D8?
C U L8R
ALGTR
(HEART FLTRS LK A SWN)
KATE

2 WHM IT MAY CONCRN
I WAN2
NETYM, NEPLCE, NEWER
ALL DA BST
BY 4 NW
NAT

PLZ CALL ME, PLZ
BCNU @ DA WKND
KATE

NAT – HAVE I GOT THE [BLUE] BOTTLE?

My head is buzzing, cannot rest
The truth is that I am obsessed.
All my daydreams sit beside her,
Me the fly and she the spider.
I should be studying, but every thought
Alights on her and then is caught
And all my hours flow and ebb
As I tremble in her silky web.
Why fear that love could suck me dry
Or that my heart will mummify?
The other girls are second best;
It's Kate who has my eyes obsessed.

Kate – Every Moment

Every stroll past empty school
And lap of pool
Every chiming of the door
And singing of the phone
Every stranger that walks by
Every minute
Every hour
Every day that flies past
I am filled with
Wonder and weightlessness
and every part of me is
Wired
For sound or sight or smell or even hint
Of you.

NAT - STORM BOY

I'm thirsty for memory of my mum, even a word,
And that phone call to my aunt stirred
Up such a storm – just had to face my fear,
Get my head and heart in gear,
Dial the number and go to meet
A real relative in a far suburban street.
And so I knocked, shocked at the end of the chase,
For the woman who answered, wore my face!
I shook like a snare drum when she hugged me,
Invited me in for a strong cup of tea,
Gave me photos and told me tales
Of how my mother softened my wails
With song. Her sweet-voiced lullaby
Was the only way to pacify –
And laid in a cot, like a dream I slept
Until the promise could no longer be kept...
And when Dad left, perhaps he wasn't a total git,
But a young lad, who couldn't cope with it.

I said goodbye, promised to keep in touch,
But this feeling inside is way too much.

NAT – THE ARGUMENT

It started when our practice was late,
Had too many beers with the boys. Forgot our date.
Next day, called by, didn't even apologise.
Played it cruel, "You know, time flies".
She lost it, screamed, cried and swore
She didn't want to see me anymore.
If this was love, it really sucked,
Well done Nat! It's self-destruct...

After hearing that my birth-mum died,
The truth is that I'm terrified –
Though I might sing a different song,
No girlfriend's ever lasted long;
For the first time Feeling shows its head,
Boxing with shadows, I knock it dead.
Abandoned is my history,
So do it before it's done to me.

Kate – Arguing With Myself

Over, over, OVER.
It is.
I am.
Over him;

Or at least I will be
Just as soon as I've thought of
The perfect put-down,
The devastating one-liner,
The public humiliation
He deserves.

Doesn't turn up, ring, text, nothing.
A whole list of did-nots
Followed fourteen hours later
By a shrug –
A shoulder movement!
No apology.
Our encounter was unblessed
With explanation.
It is so over.

CARL – THE THREAT

Are you or are you not
A very stupid moron?
Shall I just run you over a few times
With my quad bike to make sure?
You just **forgot** to tell me you were meeting Kate
After rehearsal?
Lesson one: do not miss a date.
Lesson two: If you do, grovel, eat gravel,
And work yourself to the bone to get her back again.
If you play, like you don't care,
I will have to consider castration, slowly... with a
  garlic press.
If you heed my advice (this is a threat)
Fetch forth flowers of great expense,
Get knee pads for a pilgrimage of contrition,
Scrub that dermatological hard man mask
From your face
And tell her ('cos I think you do)
That you love her.
It's just a thought,
But the species we know as "girls", have feelings too.
Now move it,
Before I insert my fretless so far up your fundament
You'll be playing 'Stairway to Heaven'
With your eyebrows!

Kate – Say It With Flowers

There were flowers,
Shoved out from a shaking hand.
I wanted to slam the door,
But he had such a hang-dog look,
How could I not fall for it?
It spilled out over tea,
All about his first family
And all that Stuff stirred up.

I've never seen a boy cry before.

Kate – Beyond The Beach

There's swimming and there's swimming –
I'm far out in the bay treading water,
The boys back on the beach on frisbee duty
Doing stuff with wind
On this perfect day.
It's funny,
But going out with Nat
Means Carl is often part of the package
(I don't mean all the time…)
I thought I'd resent it,
But we've become a sort of family.
Of course the driving helps, but he's more than that –
A real mate, a laugh, a lark, uncomplicated.
My friends are fine, but few except for Sue
And even she's fair weather, just like today.
I'm not a loner, but I like my space
And there's plenty of that here in this bay,
Deep below me, sky above.

Lunchtime,
But before that, with Carl's help –
It's time for my boyfriend to understand the meaning
Of
Wet.

34

CARL – IS IT A BIRD? A PLANE? NO, IT'S CADGE-A-LIFT-MAN!

In my rear view mirror
These two keep volleying deep glances at each other,
And I'm just the free-range pig-in-the-middle.
I can snuffle as much as I like,
But in this situation I am just the grunt,
Hauling them to and fro.
The heat today was intense as…love
With windows wound down to grab what breeze we could.
Off to the coast on route Sixty-Sex…
The road wound like a curly tail,
Following the tidal river
To finally find big water.
The perfect day!
Set up in the dunes,
Break out the windbreak,
Lay the magic carpet with parasol for instant shade.
Out there, was sizzling, bacon hot.
Nat wimping about cold water
But didn't reckon on me, Kate, Brute Force
And the subtle art of dun-king.
It's a pig, but I couldn't even drink
As we got our faces into the picnic trough.

Where did the hours go?
Within an oink of an eye,
Day departed leaving us pink and overdone,
Wallowing in a mirage of the good life.
Now, as we hit the hills of home,
The moonbeam headlights of combines
Criss-cross the fields,
Working through the stillness of night
To gather in the gold.

NAT – THE PERFECT DAY

Perhaps we take advantage of my mate
While in the back, Me and Kate
Lose our way into another world,
Where the road unwinds like a tale unfurled.
A mad and happy day, a heat-haze dream
Of gasping cold waves and laughing ice-cream.
The hours drive by way too fast,
Till the softness of twilight and we are the last
To pack up the parasol, abandon the beach
And the sea is a dream that is soon beyond reach.
This fog of wine and blanket of Kate
As we snooze in the slipstream of my best mate.

NAT - SEPTEMBER BONFIRES

In the gardens all around, summer is alight.
What's gone is being burned, and maybe that's alright.
And maybe I will not look up that name
And find the man that should burn with shame
At what he did – for that's for him to face
And I must now move on and let the chase
Go cold. For like the leaves that will turn gold
I feel such warmth and now I look ahead to hold
My Kate – though all the hazy days now flee,
I will not do what was done to me.

That's All

NAT	*Kate*
Think of this,	I think of you,
Dream	Dream,
We may be close	Am closer now
As close as air	As close as touch
Or blood or earth	Or thought or breath
Are.	Are.
We are one	We have won,
By nature	Despite nature,
Of all nature.	All our natures.
What we give	How we live
Or lose,	Or love
Is not given	Is not given
Lost,	To us,
Just is.	Just is.
Your brilliant eyes	Your blazing eyes,
Now,	Just now,
My words	These kisses
Now	flow
Are,	far
That's all	That's all.

NAT – CALLERS INTERRUPTUS

I remember at school, they taught us that sex
Could turn us into disease-ridden wrecks.
Yet to my mind, it would appear,
Without bonking, we wouldn't be here!
Now when we've gone a bit further than kissing,
I'm certain that there's something missing –
My blood like lighter fuel on fire,
Consumed by the hots as the flames creep higher.

Yesterday, when Kate's mum and dad had at last
  gone out,
We're lying on the sofa, making out,
But as items of clothing fell to the floor,
There came a sudden knock on the door!
Passion killer? It did the trick –
You've never seen garments whipped on so quick!
Just a neighbour returning a mower;
The moment was over. This wasn't a goer.
We really need to plan this better,
Or I'll end up a perpetual petter!

Kate – Burning Afternoons

It's blazed an Indian summer these past few days
Where cold, bright nights sit back to back
With burning afternoons.
And now that Nat and I can see each other every
   college day,
We spend each lunchtime in the park
And Nat pulls off his t-shirt
For us to lie back on.
And every time I see his back, his spine,
The long hips disappearing into jeans,
And when I hang my hand across his shoulders
And feel the muscle under skin, the rise and fall of ribs
The soft slide of his neck,
I know that it is good.
And when we kiss
And let our hands speak our longing
And then draw back to look and smile,
I know that it is good.
And lying there, hot with sun
And heated with the nearness and the touch
And smell and taste
And burning up with wanting
That I can hardly breathe,

We talk to break the tension,
Laugh, share silly jokes that only we could understand
And plan
The night that Mum and Dad are going to be away
And know it will be good.

I love all this: new course, new college,
People, possibility.
I love these daily changes, perfect lunchtimes
Autumn sun and most of all I love
Nat.

And of course, it goes without saying that I
Absolutely and totally, utterly, obsessively
Fancy
The
Pants off him
On a daily basis.

CARL – PLAYING THE PART OF A PARENT

CARL: I have a feeling that your loving parents are
Currently self-employed as Brush-it Undercarpet LTD,
Purveyors of special Evade-The-Issue silences
to all teenagers in a right royal huff.
So I myself, as your mate in this moral maze,
have given to undertake,
A little chat-eroni, between you and me.
(Nat groans)
I'm talking about the 'having-the-hots' moment,
The 'no-going-back-cliff-edge-wheeeeeeeeee...
   mmmmmm!' moment
Yes, it's the discussion on STD's,

NAT: Purlease!

CARL: Now, all sorts of horrid germy, virusy, very nasty
   little things
want to have a field day with your bits, or with hers or
   even with your life!
So, before your slam in the lamb, my boy,
How about a bit of a basting?

NAT: Oh god, I'm going to die of embarrassment!
Didn't we cover this in Year 10?

CARL: I don't care how you approach that packet:

tear it with your teeth, snip it with scissors, rip it in a

  fury of furnurkling

but before you, ahem, whip it in, whip It on.

Think of it as pulling down a roller blind on disease,

Fencing with a foil to pregnancy.

(I'm on a roll here).

NAT: Stop! Stop now while you can!

CARL: It's as easy as roll on, roll off like a ferry,

crossing the seas of sensual experience!

Used to be made of sheep's bladder (strange

  but true),

But now it's the latest-latex, shrink (okay,

  unfortunate choice of word there.

Where was I? Yeah.) Shrink-wrap, in Rubberwear,

Let me introduce, direct from a tour of local

  vending machines,

Appearing in your hands for a couple of quid:

The currently floppy, but soon-to-be-filled post

  of Condom!

NAT: Aarrrghhhhhhhh!

(at this point Nat is attempting to throttle Carl)

CARL – RAMIFICATIONS OF JEALOUSY

If there's one thing farmers know about,
It's breeding.
And Mr Texel, The Ram With Attitude
Is here to do the job –
Lounge lizard in designer wool.
Forget the chatup,
When you see the size of his ballot box from half a
    field away,
You know that every vote counts.
It's funny but sheep run away from you.
Cross a stile, and watch them scatter like pigeons.
But Mr Texel?
Oh no. He's a hard man.
Brick on legs with a fat face, he stares you out.
And don't you love the lingo…
It's all about servicing and tupping.
Almost sounds quaint.
But at the end of the day,
If Mr Balls-with-body-attached ain't got what it takes
(ie our flock of 300 Cambridge Ewes up the duff in
    six weeks),
he is pet food.....

Oh for the opportunity.

45

WILL — PHOTOCOPIER ENGINEER

When they ring, you wonder what lies between
   their ears.
They wail about smudges and break down in
   tears -
The office can't function, deadlines are delayed...
The machine squats smugly. They were betrayed;
And if I can't sort it, my job's on the line,
It's Photocopier Repair Man's 999.
So after I've screamed through the endless
   traffic jam,
I get there to find it's a pathetic paper jam.
Or, the poor little lady, no-one had shown her
The simple art of replacing the toner.
But don't you worry, got the lingo to impress:
"Your corona wire's gone! the thermistor's a mess!"
Take a bit of cotton and give it a clean,
Then charge the earth for fixing the machine!
And you'd think that they'd appreciate me,
Problem solved, what about some tea?
But forget it, mate, deadlines were delayed,
We'll add on some extras. Will will get paid.
Stop off for a shot and a couple of beers.
Sod the bloody lot of them. A chaser? Cheers!

ON THE RADIO ON THE WAY HOME

"This is the title track from our home grown
hip-hopper's latest album, Hemneverin."

Yeah,
This one for you guys drivin' it tonite.
Give me the beat. That's it now…

Take it, and you take it
To twoc it and let's rock it, and you clock it round
  the clock
So pump up the stereo it's time to tick tock
Grip the low fat wheel you the name checkin' boy
The boom bass in the back and the heavy alloy
From the Blackbird Leys
You're puttin' on the G's
Til you're on the run and slippin' past the ton

And you take it and to make it
With a shakin' round and round
Til the singin' of the sirens and the burnin' turnin' sound
Screamin' while you smoke, hold the toke, get the joke
  til you're high
And the boarded up houses, and the wind ridin' by

And it bypass, overpass, crossin' and you're tossin'
   and you got to get past
Take a ride, joy-ride, seek and hide and you're
   chicken too fast
Tinted in my window and chipped in my heart
I'm the turbo slag, put your foot down make a start
In the Cul-de-sac, heart-attack, no way back,
   I'm alright Jack of all ladies
Dreamer in my Beemer,
I'm the devil in designer hot wirin' it from Hades

And you take it and you fake it
And you crank it and you tank it
To the limit, of the white line, yellow line
Snort up the speed and your feelin' so fine
In the funky federation
For the guys drivin' home, it's all acceleration...

CARL – OUT OF TUNE

My mum has no sense of image.
This vehicle of hers,
has all the pulling power
of a fart at the wrong moment.

My Beautiful Bertha is squeezed in the back.
But she's not what she could be.
No-one ever had it away with a fretless bass, as far
    as I know.
Still, she's good for cuddles
and let's face it,
a band without bass is all over the place...

Natty Nat sat next to me, a smile quavering on
    his face,
off to Kate-In-Wait.
Good rehearsal...
but Nat's in for the real thing,
No hangabout fumbling at the service station –
it's the fast lane of the all-the-way-motorway.
And, she is beyond lovely. Nuf' said.
Talk about getting out of bed on the right side.
Oh, no, hang on, talk about getting into bed on the
    right side...!

I'll just go party on my tod,
and maybe with luck, end up being whipped by
  Mistress Envy.
Still,
gotta cover for my mate.
"Of course, Mrs Newbery, Nat's staying at my place
  after the party.
I'll make sure he doesn't get into trouble."

They treat me like an older brother.
But aren't older brothers supposed to get laid first
while the sibling stands back in gobsmacked awe?

Look at him there, hair sheared close,
Eyes wide, the look of a sheep about to give birth.
He's ready, ready as he'll ever be.

NAT & CARL – BANTER

CARL: Oh, my young lambikin,
Listen and learn from the man who put the 'ass' into Bass,
The 'licks' into guitar playing.
NAT: You are pure cheese, Carl!

> They see two girls, dressed up for Friday Night.
> Both: (Boyish) YEEHAH!
> Girls turn round, see car and laugh

NAT: You see, sad, sad mate. Small car. Smaller Carl!
Petite! Diminuendo! Piccolo!
CARL: Oh! I am wounded! And this from a boy only just
virgin on a new sax-life.
NAT: Exactly. While you are playing with your ring pull and
crumpling cans,
I shall be kissing my Kate.
CARL: Kissing is not the gig, I assure you. Such smooching
is merely the opening number,
the intro. Tonight, you must break free! Improvise!
Move your hands up and down her shapely scales, faster
and faster,
heaving your instrument in and...
NAT: Pur-leez! Keep your eyes on the road and hands
where I can see them!
The desperation is getting to you.
You really have been getting too fretless and fancy free!

> And around goes the banter.

FRI 26 SEPT (6.59pm)

NAT – TONIGHT

But underneath this boyish banter,
My heart's a horse! Now hear it canter.
Crappy puns and snappy smut
Sugars the twisting in my gut.
Will I be able to perform?
I'm scared to ride the bucking storm.
What if I lose my...direction,
Or suffer from premature...dejection.
Am I big enough? Will she laugh?
This worry-knife cuts me in half,
Half of longing, half of fear:
Our future seems so dark, unclear.

Yet we have talked and touched and sighed,
Tonight I shall be by her side.
My heart, a cantering, leaping horse,
My love, my Kate, we are on course.

Kate – Tonight

We are on course, my lovely lad
For moving further
Down the road of us.

Of you and me and me and you, together
Through these coming hours
Through moon and stars and blanket night
And back again to sun
And us.
There is a silence in my house.
It waits for me, for you
For foot on step and creak of door
'Till there you stand and I will touch your face,
Your hair, your neck, your lips.
Perhaps we won't know what to say
In those first moments, when we'll look away
And then glance back and smile
To see the hesitation's over.

How long now? Twenty minutes?
Maybe ten.
The teasing sounds of cars that pass,
But don't slow down

Is pain
And yet the knowing it is soon
So soon, is sweet.

There's froth of milkshake,
Fizz of shaken can
And firework fuse
That burns below my ribs.

Your head on my pillow,
Your breath on my hair,
I'll watch you sleep
And weave your scent into my sheets.

And then, tomorrow, in the mirror,
Will I change?
Hurry Nat.
I'm here and
I am waiting and
I'm waiting and
I'm loving and
I'm waiting so,
I'm waiting
Wanting
You.

CARL

The last ray of sun
Is suddenly a blinding
headlight. Bloody hell!

WILL

Bloody hell, it's been a bloody crappy day,
Bloody people in my bloody way.
A bloody job I didn't bloody need.
"Hey, dearie, bloody move it up to bloody speed!"
Why do they bloody crawl? I bloody hate
These bloodless biddies. Accelerate!
Hit the corner, at least I've got guts
As her dried up face tut-bloody-tuts!
Give the finger, see her frown
At last I put my bloody foot down.

Bloody Hell! What the hell was that?
That was close, I nearly bloody shat
Meself. Oh shit, the mirror shows
Everything. Everything slows:
A bloody silent flying car;
A tree; a crash. I've gone too bloody far
This time. Can't stop. Can't stop shaking.
They should have seen my overtaking.
I know, I'll ring nine, nine, nine...
No, someone else will, I'm sure they'll be fine,
A few bloody bruises, get a grip Will,
Just a bloody thrill and spill
But what if?... no, no, don't even think.
Tank it home. I need a bloody drink.

56

THE BUZZARD

I am honeytail, hovering, hawkeye.
Wide of wingspan, I live on the air and wait
For the far below, the lane where I feast on the fate
Of shrew and badger and fox. I cry
For my kin, but they are simply too slow,
And I, Hawkeye, am hunger-hollowed,
I dive for my dinner, the meat of the road,
And warily peck as I eye the un-natural foe.

I was hovering, honeytailed, hawkeye;
The sun now so nearly in the nest of night –
Too fast was the man with mechanical might,
His wild-eyed car, bucking as it cantered by.

I saw it all: a corner, sharpened like a claw:
He overtook with the blindness of a bat!
Man, you were mad, with your foot down flat:
The fledgelings swerved, slid, began to soar

And leaped from the earth to take wing:
Their flight cut short, they crushed into oak;
The boys now slumped and soil choked
With such shock it made my bright head ring.

This is not rabbit, mouse, or vole I cry,
But humanity, tarred and feathered with hate.
My hunger gone, for this tale I relate
Of honeytail, hovering, hawkeye.

NAT – THE ROLLERCOASTER

Have you ever come to a cliff
And the thought pops up, what if?
Or from the balcony of some high rise
Wondered if a body flies?
What lies at the end of the track?
We shake our heads, then step back.

As we leap this ancient hedge,
I fall, am falling over the edge
And all my hopes that were high-rise
Become as dust before my eyes,
Leaving just one thought: I'm late,
Too late to kiss my darling Kate.

Kate

WAITINGWAITINGWAITINGWAITINGWAITING
WAITINGWAITINGWAITINGWAITINGWAITING
WAITINGWAITINGWAITINGWAITINGWAITING
WAITINGWAITINGWAITINGWAITINGWAITING
WAITINGWAITINGWAITINGWAITINGWAITING
WAITINGWAITINGWAITINGWAITINGWAITING
WAITINGWAITINGWAITINGWAITINGWAITING
WAITINGWAITINGWAITINGWAITINGWAITING
WAITINGWAITINGWAITINGWAITINGWAITING
WAITINGWAITINGWAITINGWAITINGWAITING
WAITINGWAITINGWAITINGWAITINGWAITING
WAITINGWAITINGHATINGWAITINGWAITINGG
WAITINGWAITINGWAITINGWAITINGWAITING
WAITINGWAITINGWAITINGWAITINGWAITING
WAITINGWHEREWHATWAITINGWAITINGBIG
WAITINGWHYISHISMOBILENOTANSWERING
WORRYBLOODYHELLWAITINGWAITINGTING
WAITINGWAITINGWAITINGWAITINGWAITING
WAITINGWAITIWHEREAREYOUNATWAITING
WAITINGWAITINGWAITINGWAITINGWAITING
WAITINGWAITINGWAITINGWAITINGWAITING
WAITINGWAITINGWAITINGWAITINGWAITING

CARL – AFTERBURN

And in that moment,
When the sun turned into a burning headlight,
And I twisted the wheel with the fear of God,
We drifted slow as feathers across the road,
Found a fence,
Leaped it,
Actually flew in bright metal somersaults,
'Til a tree caught us in its arms.
Me, sober as Judgement, lolled like a boozer over
  the wheel,
Came to, turned to my best friend
Resting in his seat, silent as slaughter.
And I knew it all,
The moment I woke,
I knew it. The tree trunk, crumpling the engine
  like paper.
All our banter with its breath knocked out.
And at that moment, as I puked and shat and
  shattered my heart,
before the siren's singing began, before I passed
  out again,
All I could think of was the call, the call that had to
  be made to Kate.

PC LAURA SNEAD – THE MORE YOU DO IT

The call comes through from control.

I am the nearest, blue lamp it all the way.

Gawkers blocking the traffic.

Barrier down. One car smashed into a tree.

Assess the scene, that's what we're trained to do.

Driver seems dazed. Passenger dead.

But it's not my job to say that.

Called in. Grade 1 injury RTC.

Emergency Ambulance and Fire Brigade on the way.

Out with the slow cones,

Don't want more crashes.

As always, the public have no desire to move on.

One of them starts asking for directions, for God's sake.

Maybe I should direct him to the dead boy.

You get used to it. Part of the job. Hardened, almost.

The old dear who saw it, keeps pecking at my arm,

Going on about the purple car that sped past her.

The paramedics are checking the passenger for signs
of life

And as they help the driver into the ambulance,

It hits me. The other one.

He's the Newbery's boy.

Kate – The Phone Call

NO
NO
NO
NO
NO
NO
NO
NO
NO
NO
NO

Kate – Visit by the Family Liaison Officer

LIGHT   BRIGHT

WHAT   SOUND

DAD   MUM   HERE
         NOISE
         DOOR

UNIFORM

         SOFT VOICE   QUESTIONS

                                                  GONE

CAN'T FEEL MY HANDS   OR   FEET

WANT   MY   DADDY

WHERE'S   NAT?

DAD'S HANDS FEEL LIKE SANDPAPER.

I HATE SWEET TEA.

THIS BLANKET USED TO BE MY GRANNY'S.

THERE'S A DEAD WASP ON THE WINDOWSILL.

MY HANDS AND FEET ARE FREEZING.

THE POLICEWOMAN SMELLS OF BLACKCURRANTS.

A CORNER OF THE WALLPAPER IS CURLING. SHALL I REACH FOR IT AND TEAR?

WHERE'S NAT?

GONE.

PC LAURA SNEAD – HOW MUCH DOES A BOY'S
 HEART WEIGH?

On the Monday, I take notes,
Standing behind a screen.
There are no microphones, that's just for TV.
The mortuary is white-tiled, with ceramic tables,
Each with a draining hole.
From the fridge, the boy, identified by a tag on his wrist,
Is rolled out, trolleyed to the table.
Strange. There are no external signs of injury.
The first incision is made under the chin,
From the supra-sternal notch down to the pubis.
Observation. The chest cavity is filled with blood.
The smell? Distinctive. Have you ever been in
 an abattoir?
Or an old fashioned butcher's shop?
Dead flesh. That's as close as I can get.
The rib cage is cranked open. Organs are measured.
How much does a boy's heart weigh? I write it down
And think about my own lad, 13, crazy about cars.
The detached part of me is fascinated. How do
 people die?

64

The pathologist explains:

Hit a stationary object at 50 mph.

Everything halts, but the heart keeps beating.

The body so tense, the aorta can rip

A sudden pain as the blood leaks out into the
  chest cavity.

Dead...

Rare, but not uncommon.

The unmarked body?

You need to be alive to develop bruises.

At least it was quick.

I finish my notes, as they stitch up the unblemished boy,

Wrap him in a shroud to lie in the Chapel of Rest.

MR NEWBERY – CHAPEL OF REST

How do you identify your son?
His laugh? The pitch of his voice?
When we came here on Saturday,
We did the nodding of our heads
"That's him" we said, just like they do on TV.
And now we have some quiet time with him.
Part of me wants to clap my hands, holler
In this hallowed place, just to see him
Smirk, come to life, say "I was only joking, Dad!
  Get a life!"
I kissed him on his forehead.
I've never kissed anyone dead before.
His face quite calm, untouched,
His skin not clammy, just cold,
All that was there, not there anymore.
My wife wept and wept
And I just kept myself to myself
As you do.
But inside this Chapel of Rest, there is none.
"Come on love, there's lots to do," I said
and I put my arms around her
and with all my feeble strength
I hauled us out and away.

CARL

Neck stuck. Everything hurts.
Can't turn my head.
Can't move.
Don't want to.
Family fuss around,
Trying to feed me food I don't eat
With hot drinks that go cold.
Three hours suddenly gone.
Three minutes drag.
Can't think.
Why not me?
Why Nat?
My body is too warm,
Too much blood and life in it.

Wrong.

WILL — ON THE SICK

The night after I had given it some welly,
Guts ached, legs turned to jelly.
Through the fog of fags and booze
I tried to filter out the news.

That old biddy, her bloody fault
So slow, I almost came to a halt.
The sudden corner, poorly lit
And I am truly in the shit.
My mind is sliding into a skid
And all for a kid, a teenage kid.
One second his life was full steam ahead,
The next, thanks to me, the boy is dead.

Take my pills, I'm on the sick,
Must ignore conscience's prick.
Said they're looking for a purple car,
Garage the evidence, crawl to the bar.
Will, dead to the damning news,
Crash into a heap of booze.

CARL – THE BOY NON-RACER

You don't overtake on the inside lane with a twenty five
   year old
David Brown 780 Selectamatic, even if it does have
   twelve forward speeds.
Having driven on tractors round the farm since I was
   able to form a sentence,
I generally have a lot of respect for 3 tons of metal.
Hill too steep. Topple over. Crushed. Happened in the
   next valley,
Splurged in the local papers, then forgotten.

So I plod my way on the tarmac, A to B in country time.
But my mates, some of them...
Well, one night, out clubbing it
We hit the highway to town,
Gassing it up, stereo at full mad cow, giving it
   some Moo.
But underneath the laughs,
I was superglued to the seat.
Corners were smoothed out,
Other cars, slalom cones to be swerved round.

We got flashed, given the horn
Awarded interesting hand signals...
One near miss,
And my mates were screaming like peacocks
(if you've ever heard a peacock scream, you won't
  forget it),
too proud as they swaggered in the slipstream.

They lived to tell the tale.
But Carl, the boy non-racer,
Is the one
That gets to kill
His best friend.

Returned by the Family Liaison Officer,
With receipt:

PERSONAL EFFECTS

One guitar
One black guitar case
One small sports bag containing:
One toothbrush
One bottle mouthwash
One can deodorant
One green towel
One pair boxer shorts
One t-shirt
One black jacket
One cellophane-wrapped packet of condoms
One set of housekeys on novelty keyring
One watch
One silver earring
One leather and silver wrist-band
One folded piece A4 paper, typed song lyric
"To Kate" hand-written top left hand corner.

Kate – On Visiting Nat's House

Waiting on the doorstep
Felt like being underwater,
Kicking for the surface too far above.
And Nat's Mum stood there gaping,
Her mouth a perfect 'o', fish-like,
Forgetting how to speak.
We didn't move, each hugging our own arms
And then she said so quietly I almost couldn't hear,
"Come in Kate. Come on in. I'm glad you came."

And I tried to fix my eyes on her, just her
So I wouldn't see the details of his home
Wouldn't see his trainers
Or his writing on the calendar:
But I did.

And all the time between us,
The knowledge of what linked us:
The mother and the girl –
Both loved that boy.

We walked through to the kitchen,
Though neither of us sat, as though by standing up
We'd still hold on
And her hands plucked at the table as she
Pointed out a package
whispering
"It's for you love. Take it home."

The hug was short as we both held our tears
And I realised that the shirt she wore was his,
Crumpled, the scent already fading.

In the street,
I couldn't wait and ripped the sellotape
To find the ticking of his watch
And a song.

'TO KATE'

I'm on my way, yeah, on my way
To you, to you, to you,
Flying down that heart highway
You're my pit-stop lovin' crew.

Cruisin' through the neon night
Way down the one way street,
I got out from the cul-de sac
And it's time for us to meet.

My girl you know I'm driven,
Been so driven all my life,
Got no choice, but found my voice
To free me from the strife.

So switch on the ignition,
And power steer that wheel
Wind down all the windows
Let me tell you how I feel.

Somewhere there's a diner
That's open thru' the night
Maple syrup pancakes
You'll be my feast tonight

Cos' I'm on my way, on my way
On the lane of love to you,
Nothin' now can keep me away,
We're the non-stop kissin' crew.

Kate – The Heart's Haiku

If I could finger–
print my cold room, his touch would
   still be everywhere

MRS NEWBERY – ONE WEEK AFTER

The house hangs loose around my shoulders
As though I have grown small.
The chair is solid and the table hard beneath my hand.
I know that I'm alive
Because I hear my breaths
Beneath the cobweb of my ribs,
But that is all.
I try to summon anger but I can't
And everything I smell or taste or hear or see or touch
Is changed, is grey, is ash.
How can I eat? Wash up? Or make a cup of tea?
These things that once were normal
Now all wrong.
His clock still beeps at eight am,
And I can't turn it off, unplug it, flip the switch.
I can't do that to him yet.

Everywhere is ambush in this house –
His shirts still wait in the laundry pile,
The socks he wore discarded on the floor;
Half a pizza he said he'd finish later
Rotting in the fridge.

In his room, the duvet on his bed is cold
But if I bend to smell his pillow
He'll be there.
And if I close my eyes
I could be reaching down
To kiss my little boy
Goodnight.

Kate – Anger Lay By Me All Night Long

Bastard

Bastard

Bastard

Every stroke,

Every time my hand slices water

Every time I breathe in

And out

I'm saying it over

And over again

As I pound him

And smash him

And beat him

And drown him

The man, the coward,

The-lately-left-the-human-race

Who vanished from the scene

And sped away

With my boyfriend's soul in his boot.

Bastard

Bastard

Bastard

NAT – THESE WAYSIDE SHRINES

I am now just thought,
Living on
only in your head and the shreds
Of my mother and father.
When it happened,
It was as if all of me
Suddenly
Catapulted out into the endless sky.
I saw myself, all silent and whispered
"Oh boy!"
All that held me to the earth
Was cut away.

But I was there every day,
As you put out such flowers
By the place I left you,
Tied them to a fence
That all who drove by
Might slow for a second
and shake their heads and hearts
at what happened here.

Later,
Behind doors,
I rested in the quietness of your weeping.
Would that I could
Be a bringer of peace,
But death will not allow me.
The law of your heart must be adhered to,
And Grief your beloved now.

Kate & CARL – AT THE FUNERAL
SHELTERING IN THE MASSIVE TURNOUT

Kate: My lover now is grief. I give him flowers every day.
And as the vicar preaches
About the young promise of life
(now broken and boxed),
I cry and cling onto Carl,
who at least is breathing.

Carl: I can't breathe. I want to run, hit a field,
Lose myself, and find the man who made me swerve,
Hear the Buzzard's scream.

Kate: It's a dream, this circle completed by Nat.
But all of us sitting here only have
A date of birth and cannot know
When the circle ends.

Carl: His parents want us, his friends, to scatter
Some of his ashes in the place
He was most alive and I think of that
day by the sea,
That perfect day,
and I know he'll like it there.

Kate: There in the silence, the ticking on my wrist.
His watch still going, but his time stopped.

Carl: We're praying, but I've stopped. I can't believe.
There's nothing right
No justice in this wooden pew
I want to shout at God,
But mostly every hour, and minute and day
I blame Carl.

Kate: Carl blames himself and thinks I feel the same,
Yet I don't and I want to shake him, tell him
No! I know you're not the one who took my Nat.

Carl: Nat! Hey Nat! A bigger crowd than any gig
And you're centre stage, the main man! And
As we all file out,
Everyone says how brilliant you were,
Electric, on fire.

Kate: Water is my element,
But that won't do for you,
Now slowly consumed,
Your fire has burned my passion up
And grief is my beloved now.

CARL – OCTOBER

There's stock to feed,
Rolling and harrowing in the winter corn
And guilt.
Fences to be sorted,
(If rams can find a hole they will)
Gates re-hung
And guilt.
There's pounding in the stakes
While dad cuts and lays the hedges
But no matter how hard I hammer or how tired I get,
I'm still here, hating me.
How can Kate even bear to look at me,
The driver, survivor, not-the-boyfriend?
Police enquiries made it plain
The driver of the purple car was to blame
And leads have dried up like thistles.
But maybe I could have swerved better, or braked,
Or done that moment differently.
I dream about detective Carl, sussing out burnt
   rubber clues,
Wreaking my own brand of farmer's justice –

Stringing him up like a crow on a fence –
the gamekeeper's gibbet
To ward off vermin. Revenge
Is good for hammering out the hours,
but it can't turn back time;
No band, no songs, no banter, no one to pun with,
No best mate, no Nat.

I miss him.
At least Dad keeps me busy with my hands
But my head keeps fattening
With a glut
Of guilt.

Kate – If Only

If only

The car broke down, time slowed down, pedals were not
    pressed down,

Oh but they were.

If only

It had been a different second, minute, hour, night, road
    they had taken

But they didn't.

If only

For cancellation, hitches, postponements,

something's-come-up-I'm-delayed-by-a-bit.

If only

My Mum and Dad hadn't gone away.

But they did.

If only

I could revise, re-interpret, re-draft, disagree with,

change the outcomes of history

But I can't.

If only

It was stage-managed, improvised, stunt-doubled, that's
  a wrap!

As the actors come back to life and go home to loved
  ones

But it wasn't.

And I swim through the if-onlys

Head up and down, my arms in a constant windmill

Flailing round this pool

And if only

I left the water, and if only he was there in the shower

And if only we were kissing and alone and he unwrapped
  me like a gift…

Oh lord

If only

If only

If only

MR NEWBERY – THE SPIDER & THE FLY

After staring at the window for an hour
I heard the buzz of fly – its iridescent blue
Caught my eye and it in turn was caught by a spider
Less than half its size.
The beating of its wings soon stilled,
A small, deliberate death.
For a second,
I forgot myself,
Forgot the man whose name I might never know
Who drove too fast
And in the slipstream stole my son away.

Apparently, some who lose a limb still feel it's there –
Convinced that vanished fingers flex,
Wonder at the ghostly wriggle of a toe.
And I believe my Nat's still here
Behind that door, just waiting for his tea
While grumpy me goes on about a plate that's
    going cold.
It's all gone cold now
And the boy we borrowed for a while has been
    returned

And I want to shake the man I do not know
Shake him till his shoulders crack,
Feel the buckling of his knees
And say to him,
It's speed and speed and pedal down
And spinning of this world too fucking fast
That spun my boy from me.

Kate

My mates at college
Still aren't good on death.
I know they tried
But I remember
When I first saw Sue,
After,
Her eyes slid away
And though her lips tried hard with a
"So sorry when I heard,"
You could see her feet were itchy,
Desperate to get away.
At least with Carl
We share the subject of our silence
And if there is any ease to be felt,
I can feel the edge of it with him.

MRS NEWBERY

I found his snuggly this afternoon.
I little bit of an old nightie,
But the best security blanket he ever had.
How he used to scream if it was lost – the
House had to be turned upside down –
And no other bit of cloth would do.
Yes, he felt like mine,
Though I never bore him,
Never would a child, any child, ever.
But I so wanted to give my love.
So I did, and the process! The forms and the interviews,
You would think we were murderers in disguise!
Guilty until proved innocent.
But when we finally had him,
He was an innocent lamb,
Beautiful
And we gave him everything we had –
At least I can say that - though we never hid
His past from him.

It's funny, but after I gave him the birth certificate,

He went quiet, but I thought to myself,

That's his business now

And was secretly scared.

And maybe I should search, at least to let his other
   mother know.

Know what? Give her the grief that I must carry now?

No. That's all gone with him.

And I'm left hugging his snuggly tight.

Kate – Loose Change

I feel a bit like one of those decorative fruit bowls
People put on their dining tables:
Empty at first
But slowly filling up with bits and bobs
The fluff and rubber bands,
Loose change and dusty clutter
Of days which follow days.

I remember people telling me
"Life goes on Kate." And hating them like hell.
But of course, it has, in unexpected ways.
It's the mundane stuff which most surprises me;
Teeth still need brushing,
Cat wants feeding,
Mum still leaves me lists:
'Empty dishwasher, sign xmas card, ring if you need
    picking up.'
The card bit is hard, too many rosy-cheeked smiles.

I catch the bus to college,
Catch a cold,
Catch up with coursework,

Catch up with casual mates:

> Idle banter
> Trivial gossip.

I only talk with Carl.
For ages he wouldn't drive a car
Hated even being driven,
Until his biggest brother forced him,
Round the fields and finally,
Along the lanes.
Carl said I should do the same with Nat's C.D –
The one of all their songs;
Face it, face the voice preserved for ever.
But I can't – can't fit it in the slot,
Press play and hear him where he'll never change.

And so I play my other music loud
And catch the bus to college
Day by day.

MRS NEWBERY

No-one
Will
Ever
Call
Me
Mum
Again.

CARL – JANUARY

As I walk with Kate and see
The sheep adopt a camouflage of snow
And flail in drifts,
As we pass the cows in barns
Now stalled,
Their breath rising like tethered steam engines
As we spy
The snowdrops braving white,
Despite
The numbness of the day,
And as we tumble into the farmhouse
And warm our hands with
sweet strong cups of tea
I have the sense
That life
Goes
On

Kate

Tonight,
When I got into bed,
I realised I had spent a whole day
Without thinking of Nat,
Once.
After college in the café,
I even found myself
Creased with laughter
At Carl's over the top (and they really are!) puns.
So that's twice I've caught myself out –
Not in the thick of missing him.
It feels strange
I almost want to own up to someone,
Admit my guilt –
Afraid that letting go of constant sadness
Might mean
Letting go of Nat.

CARL – SPRING

Global warming doesn't get a look in up in these hills.
The first lambs plopping out all over the place,
While outside, it's a blizzard.
So the world goes on.
My neck still stiff - apparently I could get compensation...
If they found the driver.
But no banknote can fill me up now.
I sometimes see the Newberys, stop to talk.
They're great at brave faces,
But when they see me,
It's like inserting a memory stick.
All they want is gossip about our old gigs,
And school, and what we used to get up to,
Keeping their son on the go with my words.
Kate can't handle visiting them anymore.
We seem to be hanging out a lot
and she keeps giving me a hard time about the band,
saying I should get it together again.
I don't know,
But as I was driving away yesterday,
suddenly he was sitting in the seat beside me:
The old Nat in his beat-up leather jacket,
Giving me the wink.

And then he was gone,
Off on another road trip I wouldn't be joining.
Go for it, mate.
I hope they like your lyrics up there.

Kate – At The First Reformed 'Stormboy' Gig

Considering the room's so cold,
I'm hot,
Hoping Carl will be okay up there.
I'm not sure I can watch,
But know I must.
Sue said she'd stay,
Make sure I'm not alone.
Although I always am
With anyone who doesn't understand.
Time doesn't fly.
It swims,
And now I'm here,
And Carl has written a new song
And some other wild-armed lead guitar
Will sing the lyrics of my Nat.
My Nat? He's not mine anymore, not anyone's,
Though I always carry him with me.
It still hurts, maybe it always will,
An ache I am slowly learning to live with…

I can tell that Carl is nervous on the bass,
But as the band kicks in,
Considering the room's so cold,
I'm not…
alone.

CARL'S SONG – THE BURGLAR

Listen, let's set up the job,
And pray it's in the bag,
Hope there are no witnesses,
As I steal away the swag.

Today I will betray the law
With my illicit needs,
In my heart a master key
For sensual proceeds.

Judge, jury sentence me,
Check out that girl's history,
What shall I plead, lady?
Tattoo me with a Guilty.

When I see ya walkin' by,
Wonder what's the point,
Cos I know that you're not mine,
As I'm casin' up the joint,

Muscle in, tread on those toes,
You're givin' me such grief,
Can I get away with you?
The original Love Thief.

Judge, jury sentence me,
Check out that girl's history,
What shall I plead, lady?
Tattoo me with a Guilty.

My bank account is empty,
No diamonds, no fast car.
What I need's reality,
No need to wish upon a star.

Maybe I'm just a swindler,
Baby, catch me if you can.
Solitary confine my soul,
But hope for the Highwayman.

Judge, jury sentence me,
Check out that girl's history,
What shall I plead, lady?
Tattoo me with a Guilty.

WILL – SELF WILL & THE CALL

I'm good at leaving things behind,
But still I carry them in my mind.
The job's gone. Thanks to a doctor's note,
I'm fulfilling my destiny as a scumbag scrote.
That lad sits in my head every day,
And no amount of lager takes him away.
And when I wake up without warning,
Retching bile at three in the morning,
I suddenly fall back through the years
To a wailing baby and a torrent of tears...
Another time, another place,
When I wore that younger face
Of scared-boy Billy, the lad who ran
And so my double life began.
I'm just a copy of my former self,
With seventeen years of the past on the shelf.

Where are they now? If only I could see,
Just for one second, my real family.
As my head lolls against the loo,
A voice says, "To thine own self be true."
Choices: now the truth has come too close,
Deny and fly with an overdose?
Or: bottle it out, who'll ever know?
Start again (again) — Will on the go.
Or: sober up and pray to surprise
The world by putting down the lies?
Guilt in my gut, a phone on the wall,

Will Will lift it and make that call?

CARL

I've never tried to two-time a ghost before.
Getting my head round this is like trying to bend ice –
It cracks me up.
My dad always takes the bullseye point of view –
Steak on legs doesn't have confidence issues
Or worry whether Miss Cow fancies a bit of meat and
   two veg...
But knowing my luck,
My attempt will end up like a bull in a china shop.
Getting the horn only causes trouble...
I mean, we've grown close,
Close as almost every thought and feeling shared,
Close enough maybe to just
Lean my head and...
Sheepish Carl and Kate, the new Ewe on the block?
Oh! It seems so far-fetched. Who am I kidding?

What's Nat got to say?
He's mostly quiet these days.
But he's still my best mate
And I miss him like crazy.
Can the dead be jealous? Dead jealous.
Yeah, I can hear
Him turning in his grave,
Sick to death of my awful puns.

But he's not here and I am.
And if these living arms are strong enough
To wade into the womb
And pull that mess of slimy lamb to
Plop to the earth and be licked by a mother into life,
Then these living arms
Are strong enough
To wrap around this girl.

Kate – Lambing Time

Carl invited me over for the lambing.
I love all the tumbling buildings
Gently sinking into the dusk.
Everything is too neat and tidy these days.
Under the curved corrugated roof, the wind was stilled
And for a second I felt humbled –
Like those shepherds at the manger
The sight of the new-borns tottering and swaying like grass.
The effort they made to get up! To live!

One ewe looked uncomfortable,
Just sat there, broken waters spilling around her.
Typical Carl:
"This calls for the Lubrel and a bit of
gruesome gynaecology girl! Close your eyes if you're
    sheepish!"
He smiled and covered his arm in gel and in he went.

He had some thick electrical wire twisted into a
  rough noose,
"It's all about feeling!" he grunted
but then he got the head and feet and pulled
and out slid a mass of woollen slime.
How could something like that ever live?
Carl stuck his finger in its nose to pull the mucus out
And grabbed the back legs to swing the lamb
Round like a lead weight.
I was horrified,

But then it coughed and Carl so gently put it
By the ewe, who began to lick away the slime.
He looked at me then
And I thought,
Well,
Maybe.

AFTERWORD

In local papers every week, brief details are reported: road accident injuries, deaths, times, types of vehicle, crashes, smashes, names and ages. Behind each name, we know there's a story, but mostly, we just don't want to go there. Move on, keep moving, don't dwell on it.

The initial idea for this novel in poems grew slowly. First, there were the car journeys. Mad drivers overtook on blind corners, where we prayed nothing was coming in the opposite direction. Several times, we were the 'something' innocently coming the other way, braking, swerving, only just avoiding... what if...? What if...? What if we'd started out a few seconds earlier...? Then there were our children, our pets, narrowly missed by (what shall I call them?) Boy racers? Well, not just boys, but those for whom speed is an ego trip, show off, power thing. And the flowers. Flowers laid on grass verges, tied to fences, resting in hedges. There are so many flowers, marking someone's vigil, someone's loss.

There was a kind of rage building up in us at the selfishness, the "outta my way sucker", the "don't give a damn" self-importance that steps hard on the accelerator.

Give a damn. Look at those roadside flowers. Imagine the story behind them. That's how 'Crash' came to be written. The characters we made up are rooted in every story behind every wayside bouquet. Nat, Kate, Carl, the others, they're all part of imagining what if...? What if...? Most of the time, we don't want to go there. But every day, someone does.

THESE WAYSIDE SHRINES

These wayside shrines
Stations of the metal cross
Are moments when a man is mad,
His head, a river of rush,
Depression of the clutch
And the push too far, too fast
The flowering of flame.
Life, metallic on the tongue,
Is tasted, then spat out.
And what of the innocents? What of them,
At the moment when a salesman, an angry man,
An over-taking superman with St Vitus in his toes,
At the moment when he daubs his cross
On the innocent's door?
How they gather wings unto themselves
To launch through windscreens,
Break upon the air,
Death wrapped round them like Jacob's ladder,
With no glance down,
They are gone.

And these wayside shrines,

These bouqueted markers

Where all of a family's rage is wrapped in cellophane

They make us pause,

For a second, slow ourselves

As we also spiral upwards

Into the blue places where we talk with spirits;

And behind, and below

The steel lament, of wives, of husbands, of all lovers

Left in the rend and rip of days,

Cats-eyes weeping

At these wayside shrines.

Statistic: the leading cause of death among children and young people under the age of 25 is ROAD ACCIDENTS.